Memoirs Of Love

A collection of poems by Johnnethia Paige Solin

Memoirs Of Love

A collection of poems by Johnnethia Paige Solin

JASHER PRESS & CO.

Published By:
Jasher Press & Co.
P.O. Box 14520
New Bern, NC 28561

Copyright© 2012
Interior Text Design by Pamela S. Almore
Cover Design by Pamela S. Almore

ISBN: 978-0615591520
Memoirs of Love: A Collection of Poems by Johnnethia Paige
Solin

First Edition
Printed and bound in the United States of America

Dedication

I dedicate this book to my Heavenly Father who has given me the ability to be a ready writer. I thank Him for years of protection, love, and friendship.

To my husband, thank you for being my Hero. Thank you for loving me and not giving up on me. For I have found the one my heart loves.

To my mom Teresa who travailed in birth with me and who labored in love through the years to take care of me. If it was not for your sacrifices, I would not be the person I am today. Thank You.

To my family, thank you for being a part of me. I will always be a Paige at heart. To the years of laughter and tears, I have experienced with you, I will always remember. To all of you, I Love You.

To my friends who have stuck closer to me than a brother, I thank God for every one of you. Whether you have been a friend for a season or a lifetime, thank you for the time you shared in my life.

To the Shepherds of God who have watched over me in my walk with Christ, thank you for the life changing words from God and impartations you gave me.

And last, but not least, thank you to the many readers who will read and support this work. May your hearts be encouraged.

Remember to guard your heart with all diligence, because out of it flows the issues of life (Proverbs 4:23).

Contents

Purpose   9
Introduction   11
Love   13
A New Day   15
Joy Unspeakable   17
What's the Glory   19
Trust   21
Heeding The Voice of God   23
To Go or Not to Go   25
Choose   27
Separated   29
Eternal Life   31
Granny's Life   33
Pain   35
Tears   37
My Husband   39
You   41
The Pen of a Ready Writer   43
Love Again   45
Alabama   47
The Beauty of Love Unfolding   49
Come   51
Ne-Ne   53
To My Pat   55
The Beauty of Jesus   57

Purpose

The purpose of this book (collection of poems) is to encourage the body of Christ. Each poem is written from the heart of God. May you read these poems and know that God will send you help from the sanctuary and strength out of Zion (Psalms 20:2).

Introduction

Walking as new creatures in Christ, there are times where we will have different seasons of trials, test, and tribulations. Whether they are emotional, spiritual, relational, or financial, there will always be a word from God to strengthen our hearts.

From the time I have walked as a believer of Jesus Christ, there have been different situations to try my faith, test my love for Christ, and develop my patience. Out of these trying times I would write from my heart. I pray this book will encourage you in your walk with God, as it has encouraged me.

Always remember when you have done all to stand, stand therefore anyhow (Ephesians 6:13).

Love

L ove, a gift that only God can bring;
A way of life that everyone should claim.
A desire to be fulfilled in everyone's heart
A feeling that can bring life or death-
Life if nurtured. Death if forsaken.
A force so powerful-
The strength of a mighty bomb'
Yet so delicate and tender.
How could it break a person's heart?
To experience love is a dream come true;
To misuse love no one should do.
With everything in the world to dream to have-
Love is the one, I want to come true.

8-13-02

A New Day

Behold! A new day has come.
Rise for the Glory of the Lord is upon you.
Remember ye not the former things of old
neither consider your past.
For this day I will do a new thing in you.
Why are you looking back?
Eyes have not seen, ears have not heard,
Nor has it entered into your heart, the things
I have in store for you.

7-30-02

Joy Unspeakable

O h! What a beautiful smile you exemplify. What a beautiful radiance that shines so brightly from your face.
Maybe it's from the new job you
just acquired; or maybe that cute guy/girl just told you hi.
But I see it from you everyday.
Could it be the new found love you have acquired with Christ Jesus that has filled you
with joy unspeakable.
Look how it has changed you.
Yes, keep walking in this extraordinary, unheard of place that man can not give you.
But guess what?
They cannot take it from you either.
It is a gift bestowed upon you from your Heavenly Father.
Bask In It.

7-28-02

What's the Glory

The glory of God is the awesomeness of God.
It is the majestic fragrance of a risen savior
that holds the entire world in His hand.
It is the pureness of the only Holy Priest
given to mankind.
It is the sweet innocence of a virgin birth lad
that came to save earth.

7-30-02

Trust

Trust in the Lord with all thine Heart.
Ever wanted to know what was God going to do?
Instead of trusting that God is going to do it or already has, you exhaust your mind and spirit to figure things out.
Why must we know every move or the next step we are going to make, when we say we trust a God that already knows every move and every step we take before we even take them.
Trust is not you knowing something, but knowing God knows and knowing He has you covered.
Sit. Acknowledge Him and then trust in Him.

7-28-02

Heeding the Voice of God

E ver wondered what was that desire that
would never leave you or where that
"suddenly one day" thought came from?
Maybe it was a coincidence or it was just
a brilliant idea from you. Or could it have been a
leading from your Heavenly Father.
When you are one with Christ, you can trust that
our Heavenly Father will not lead us astray.
For He knows the path we will travel and He has
already gone before us (that way). Maybe it
was a desire to move to a new city, or to start a new
ministry, or even to visit an old friend. Do
those things you hear in your spirit. Follow the
promptings of the Holy Spirit within you and
trust God is there with you.

7-28-02

To Go or Not to Go

There has been an inward call to you that says, "Go".
There has been a burning desire that will not be quenched that says, "Get there".
But there has been outward circumstances, outward voices, and fear that says it couldn't be.
You begin to listen to the voices of reasoning, the voices of doubt, the voices of confusion and so you decide it wasn't anything at all.
You try to go on as usual, but that inner call comes back again and says, "Go".
You ask, "What do I do"?
Ever wondered what the voice of the Holy Spirit sounds like? You guess right!
Follow that prompting. It is the Holy Spirit calling you from your present place.
He wants to do a new thing with you.
Shall ye not know it?

7-28-02

Choose

C hoose ye this day whom you will serve.
Why keep playing with your eternal
destination?
There is a Heaven and there is a hell.
Every man will be judged according to his sin.
Whatsoever you sow, you shall reap.
Choose ye today life that you and your household
may live.

7-30-02

Separated

S eparate unto me Paul and Barnabas for the work in which I have called them to.

Ever wonder why you never seem to fit:
Why is it so hard for me to join this group
or this club, you might ask?
Ever wonder why it seems as if when in a big
crowd you still feel alone? No, you are not weird.
Take courage. God says you are not alone. For He
has separated you. He has put a shield of protection
around you. He has you in a place unto Himself,
where only He can sit and dwell.
Appreciate this place and learn of Him.
Remember there is no elevation without separation.

7-28-02

Eternal Life

Today is the day my grand-daddy said goodbye.
But tomorrow will be the day he will meet God in
the sky.
There he will converse with God of all the things he did in
his life.
There it will be determined if he will have eternal life.
Only God knows why He called my grand-daddy home and
only God knows where his soul will make its home.
Will it be home in the bosom of Christ or will it be there in
the valley of Sheol?
Please, today, you have the choice to see my grand-daddy
again.
Please, today, let Christ in.
Know, today, that our lives are but a twinkle of an eye.
Please know, today, where you will spend eternal life.

6-4-03

Granny's Life

83—The number of Granny's Life
8—New Birth, New Beginnings-A New Creation
3—Resurrection, Divine, Completeness, Perfection

Granny has been given a new beginning. She now has the wonderful new life with Christ we are all looking forward to seeing one day. God the Father has resurrected Granny's Spirit unto Him and now she is complete. She is standing there before the father in His divine perfection. She is now seated in Heavenly Places with Christ Jesus. So please don't look as if Granny is gone—no she is only at home. A place no man can go without knowing Jesus Christ. So as Granny's name, "Ida Bell Anderson" was recorded in the Lambs' book of life and she was a chosen vessel unto God, remember her spirit and how she loved God. Follow in her ways and one day we will all see the Father. Remember, to be absent from the body is to be present with Christ (our Lord).

Father we love you,
Granny we miss you,
Love Always,
Johnnethia Y. Paige—great-grandchild

5-26-01

Pain

Why must I feel the pain inside?
How can I explain what's on the inside?
The trials of my life I don't understand.
The heartache—I can't contain.
At time it feels as if I'm not loved.
At times I feel as if I'm to blame.
Who can I talk to? Who can help
bear this pain? I pray to God
for a shoulder to lean on. I pray to
God for someone who sees me—
as the creation God created me, but
at times I feel it's Him who does this to me.
How much longer I think. How much more
must I endure-loneliness, unhappiness, this facade of
a smile and my inner man feels like Hell? The tears that
I shed; at times I can't even think.
Sitting in this room just me alone without a number to call.
So I sit here with my pen and write what I feel.
All in all praying God will deliver me from this pain.

9-15-03

Tears

W hat are the small droplets of water that fall from your eyes?
Is it the sign of your life story? Does it tell what's going on with you?
Maybe it shows someone-they can help you.
Never hold your tears inside. Never allow your heart to become stopped up.
For tears are a cleansing for your soul.
Tears are a release of pain and signs of joy.
Never come to a point where you can't cry.
Never allow your natural release to stop.
Know that every tear you release is not lost.
For your Heavenly Father holds them in a vial.

9-15-03

My Husband

My husband is the man God has for me.
My husband is the protector over me.
My husband is the King of our abode, no doubt.
He is the chosen vessel to lead me out.
He is the visionary of our home.
He is like marrow to a bone.
Without his leadership, I cannot follow.
Without his presence, why even bother?
Without his seed, a generation could be lost.
Without his smile, my heart cries out.
To have a husband is a blessing from God (a dream come true).
To have a man that represents God in front of you.
Know, my husband, there is no else like you.
Know, my husband, my love is for you.
Know, my husband, the vows I took are until the end,
Know, my husband, you will always have a friend.
Look up my King and follow Christ.
Look behind you and see your wife.

Love Love

11-13-02

You

So it's you I've been praying to God about.
It's you I've been waiting to be connected to.
My prayers have gone into the atmosphere and have
helped watch over you and I thank my God I've finally
had the chance to meet you.
I'm so blessed my Lord heard my prayers and preserved
you.
I'm so delighted in the masterpiece He has created you.
A tall, brown, handsome man. A Holy Ghost filled, tongue
talking, praying man. A man after God's own heart.
A man delighted to do the will of God.
There's no other place I'd rather be right now, cause if
I step out of time I might have missed my appointed time.
My appointed time to meet the man of my dreams,
my appointed time to share my dreams.
Our lives will be a testimony for the Lord Jesus Christ.
Our love will be a fulfillment of His Grace. Remember the
words He said to you, remember the visions He gave you.
Know that at all times I am here for you.
Know at all times I'll be praying for you.
Rise up my Prince and take your throne.
Rise up my lord and heed the call.
Walk in dominion, power, and authority.
Take the lead and save the nations.
I know you are called to fight against hell

but I know you will prevail.
So whatever life brings your way from this
day forward,
Always remember you got your wife.

From the throne room of Heaven,
Your Princess,
Ne-Ne

9-12-03

The Pen of a Ready Writer

The pen of a ready writer is a gift from God.
It's the ability to hear and write the script down.
It flows from another being.
It's like an outside force that tells you when.
You always stand guard because you never know
when it may fall.
You just hope there's a pen and pad around.

9-16-03

Love Again

Yes, it's time for you to blossom within.
Yes, it's time for you to love again.
I know someone you trusted broke your
Heart and you can't imagine going through
that pain again, but this time around I promise
it won't be the same.
Love is gentle, love is kind, love is a treasure to be found.
Remember ye not the former things of old.
Remember ye not the lies that were told.
Open your heart and watch the magic unfold.
For the greatest gift of God is about to be shown.
God is truly about to send the right one your way,
but you must be open to recognize their face.
Their face will have the Spirit of God, there speech
will be the voice of God.
So this day I tell you trust again- sit back, relax, and love
again.

9-19-03

Alabama

A labama, is the place where I grow old,
The place where the "Tide" rolls.
Sunny skies which brighten my days
makes me feel like I'm in my youth again.
The smell of crisp bacon and home grown eggs
makes me smile and sigh out loud.
Beautiful clouds which cover the sky
can hide a rich history that surrounds our home.
From the days of segregation to "American Idol"
Oh Wow!
Yes, Alabama is home to me,
only I can tell how sweet it can be.
Come visit this place and see this Dixie land
you can sit under one of our "Southern Longleaf Pines",
or maybe visit Botanical Gardens and smell a "Camellia"
divine, or maybe just look up in the sky and see a
"Yellowhammer" pass by.
Whatever you choose to do, will be just fine.
So come on and visit this great state of mine.

10-5-03

The Beauty of Love Unfolding
(Part II)

As I write this poem, I write this poem for you. I remember the words you once wrote, and now I'm writing part II.

The Beauty of Love Unfolding

The Beauty of Love Unfolding (Part I) had nothing to do with me. It was a poem of love written by you, for a love that was untrue.
The beauty of love you once had is enclosed deep within. Now you are scared to trust again. Scared to place your heart into someone else's hand.
The true beauty of love, is the opportunity to love something or someone new; without remembering the ugliness of a facade of love given to you.
The true beauty of love is tearing down walls in front of you.
It's digging through the dirt and mire to find the diamond hidden within.
It's allowing your heart to become free and loving again.
The true beauty of love is fresh, pure, and clean. Untainted by those who doesn't know how to treasure its' gifts and its' dreams.

The Beauty of Love Unfolding

It's the innocence of saying I Love You while holding hands.
It's the glare in ones' eyes while admiring their smile.
It's the first kiss shared by two, whose passion has arise.

49

It's the quickening heartbeat and the fluttered sound.

Aww...The Beauty of Love Unfolding

It's the thoughts in your mind that are secretly revealed.
Too shy to respond, but desperately wanting to.
It's the faith filled prayers whispered at night to God up
above.
Asking Him to bring your hearts together and waiting
patiently until He does.

The Beauty of Love Unfolding

I could go on and on, but as I close this poem,
I hope you remember the words I have written.
If you really want to see the beauty of love unfold-
watch the beauty of love unfold within you.

Year of our Lord 2003

Come

Deep within I hear this call again
saying come, come, come, come be my friend.
There is no way this voice could mean me.
Why me? At times this terrible being on the
inside of me. It tells me to do things I can't
even mention. It makes me feel like a second
class creature. Is there anyone, anyone who
understands what I am saying? Is there anyone who can
tell me how to get rid of this other dimension inside of me?
Free, Free, Free, Free I would like to be.
But instead, I'm bound by an unseen force that's bigger
and sometimes gets the best of me. I cry out and say
Oh Lord help me! I wonder if He ever hears me.
That inside being clouds my mind and says it can't be.
Then, I hear this call again, saying come, come, come,
Come be my friend.

12-11-03

Ne-Ne

This southern grown petite me
    This chocolate girl they call Ne-Ne.
    A wonderful work God has done
on the inside of me.   A creature
He has created to represent His kingdom.
Prayer birthed on the inside of me
Destiny manifesting before me.
"Go forth my child and show love"
is what He told me.
Exhort, encourage, and Matthew 25:24-40
is a key verse He gave me.
A heart of flesh He gave me.
Changing me from the stony rock
the enemy designed for me to be.
What a wonderful change my life
has taken since I accepted Jesus Christ to
live inside me.

12-11-03

To My Pat

Written for Mrs. Patricia Coteat Burns
Passed away 4-14-04

Thank you for the years of caring for me.
You knew me before I knew me.
Thanks for being there to listen to my cries.
From years of infancy, adolescence, teen-age, to adulthood.
You poured so much into me, years and years of just being
there for me.
You taught me so much, just as a mother would.
From girl talks, guy talks, even tips on motherhood.
Not too many people are willing to teach you how to cook,
but you showed no hesitation in being a taster of my dishes.
My heart misses you and will miss you deeply.
Every remembrance I have of coming over and falling
asleep under your coffee table as a child,
to sitting on the porch with you hours at a time,
to scrubbing your back while you bath,
from pinching your hinder part as you walk by.
There is so much I could share, I just thank my God
for allowing us to be in each other lives.
I pray now He enjoys you even more than what I have.

Love Always,
Your Black JuJu

4-18-04

The Beauty of Jesus

The beauty of Jesus
So kind so innocent
The purest spirit of all
The magnificent brilliance of all mankind
The inner being sanctified with oils of myrrh
His tears so clear, showing love for us all.

Memoirs Of Love

A collection of poems by Johnnethia Paige Solin

About the Author

Johnnethia P Solin, born Johnnethia Yvonne Paige was born and raised in Birmingham AL. She is the only child to Teresa Paige (Kelley) and Johnny Moore. Johnnethia, better known as "Ne-Ne" graduated from University of Alabama at Birmingham with a BS degree in Respiratory Therapy in 2001. In 2002 she moved to Columbus OH to attend World Harvest Bible College. There she met and fell in love with her husband Anthony Patrick Henry Solin. They currently have 3 beautiful children.

Johnnethia is also president and founder of a private foundation, Love Love Foundation, Inc. Love Love was birthed into her heart Sept. 26, 2001. Love Love's purpose is to touch lives in need with the Love of Jesus Christ. Johnnethia currently resides in Jacksonville NC.

Contact Information

www.ajsolin.org
info@ajsolin.org
johnnethia@yahoo.com

www.ingramcontent.com/pod-product-compliance
Lightning Source LLC
Chambersburg PA
CBHW031528040426
42445CB00009B/440